The

Of The Bible

"7 Most Infamous"

By Boomy Tokan

The Bad Boys Of The Bible

"7 Most Infamous"

©2013 Boomy Tokan

Table of Contents

Introduction v
Chapter One: Doeg the Edomite 1
Chapter Two: Abimelech 7
Chapter Three: Ziba 13
Chapter Four: Achan 19
Chapter Five: Judas Iscariot 25
Chapter Six: Baanah and Recab 31
Chapter Seven: Ananias and Sapphira 37
Conclusion... 43
Other Books By Boomy Tokan...................................... 47

Introduction

We were getting the church hall ready for Sunday Service late that Saturday night when our conversation went towards the Bible and some of my books. My sister, Andette Veroudon, spoke up (in her Dutch accent with a hint of African although she is Caucasian), saying, "Sir, why don't you write about the bad boys of the Bible too, as a follow up to your Bad Girls of the Bible book?"

That was a light bulb moment because I was not thinking about such a title until that moment. We quickly began to mention prospective names to research for the book, some obscure and some more obvious.

As we walked into the house we found my wife doing one of the things she loves most in life— ironing clothes (she recently bought a brand new Hinari Digital Steam Iron she was trying out!).

We told her about our conversation and she got excited. Biblical names were rolling off her tongue (she is not only a beautiful woman, great singer and ironer of clothes, but a woman of the Word too). For example Ziba made it into this book because of her.

Over the next few days, and during my time at the Pilgrims Hall Retreat Centre, I typed on my laptop and this book is the result.

By the time you read this it would have passed through my two daughters for editing; ever faithful Jennifer Serwa "Sledge" Manuh; wise and enthusiastic Daisy Mweru; and my wonderful Sister in CHRIST, Ope! Well, none of this would be possible without my real supporters; they are the ones who buy, review and encourage the writing process, along with the members of my Facebook page.

A big thank you to you all.

JESUS is LORD!

Boomy Tokan

Contact Me Directly

Email: admin@boomytokanministries.com

Join My Fan Page Facebook page:

http://tinyurl.com/facebook-Boomy-Toka

Chapter One: Doeg the Edomite

Scripture - 1 Samuel 21: 7, 22: 6-23 & Psalm 52

Doeg may be unknown to many but his wickedness, greed and murderous instinct earns him a top seven position among the Bad Boys of the Bible.

He singlehandedly killed eighty-five priests and put to death the residents of Nob (the town of the priests) killing all its men, women, children and infants, including cattle, donkeys, and sheep! Only GOD knows what made Doeg the way he was.

Whether it was his background, family upbringing or the environment he grew up in. We do know he was an Edomite and that Saul waged war and defeated them as mentioned in 1 Samuel 14: 47. Perhaps Doeg escaped the sword of Saul or he was one of those aliens residing in Israel; we are not told.

Interestingly, there are only a few verses that give us an insight into who he was, but the Scripture is very clear about what he did, how he thought, who he associated with, and the raw perversion that existed within his mind.

Let's pick up Doeg from the first Scripture that introduces him in the Bible:

1 Samuel 21: 7: *"Now one of Saul's servants was there that day, detained before the Lord; he was Doeg the Edomite, Saul's head shepherd."*

Then 1 Samuel 22: 9-10: *"But Doeg the Edomite, who was standing with Saul's officials, said, "I saw the son of Jesse come to Ahimelech son of Ahitub at Nob. 10 Ahimelech inquired of the Lord for him; he also gave him provisions and the sword of Goliath the Philistine."*

and **1 Samuel 22: 18-19:** *"18The king then ordered Doeg, "You turn and strike down the priests." So Doeg the Edomite turned and struck them down. That day he killed eighty-five men who wore the linen ephod. 19 He also put to the sword Nob, the town of the priests, with its men and women, its children and infants, and its cattle, donkeys and sheep."*

Who is Doeg?

Doeg rose to the position of head shepherd probably after a long tenure of service and the display of loyalty and trust worthiness to Saul. This position ensured he travelled around with Saul and stayed amongst the high ranking officials of the king. He went to Nob, the town of the priests, to worship and overheard a conversation between Ahimelech and David.

He reported this to Saul after the pitiful "Nobody cares about me speech" that Saul gave. Saul called for the priest who arrived with eighty-six of his family members.

After a short interrogation and the honest reply by the priests, Saul decided they should all die. He ordered the guards at his side to turn and kill the priests after accusing them of siding with David. The guards had reverence for GOD and would not do it.

Saul must have noticed that Doeg had no fear of GOD and asked him to do the killing. Doeg killed eighty-five (one escaped). His bloodthirsty appetite needed no encouragement from Saul because, all by himself, he decided to eradicate the whole town of Nob. He killed the newly born children as well as defenceless men and women.

This was his final act and final mention. David correctly documents the actions of Doeg in **Psalm 52.** I really believe **vs. 2-3 and 7** sum up who Doeg was. The Bible says:

" *Your tongue plots destruction; it is like a sharpened razor you who practice deceit. 3 You love evil rather than good, falsehood rather than speaking the truth. Selah 4 You love every harmful word, O you deceitful tongue!... 7 Here now is the man who did not make God his stronghold but trusted in his great wealth and grew strong by destroying others!"*

What made Doeg one of the most infamous?

1. 1. **He was a cold-blooded murderer.** He went on a killing spree, killing the defenceless and innocent without any remorse whatsoever. It is logical to think that the evil spirit that was at work in Saul's life also had a firm hold on Doeg. This possession of evil drove him to murder a whole town!

2. 2. **He had no fear of GOD.** Although Doeg went to Nod the priests' town and spent time with Ahimelech, his heart was not touched by the activities he did. Surprisingly, men much stronger than he refused to kill the priests but not Doeg! The Bible assures us that *"the fear of the LORD is the beginning of wisdom"* (Job 28: 28, Psalm 111: 10 & Proverbs 9: 10). The problem is that people can do absolutely anything if they lack the fear of the LORD. This is another reason Doeg is one of the infamous Bad Boys of the Bible.

3. 3. **Doeg did anything to please an evil boss.** 1 Samuel 22: 7-8 details a most pathetic speech. In his words Saul assumed that Jonathan had sided with David against him. He further accused Jonathan of inciting David to lie in wait against him. Only a sick mind like Doeg's could yield to such words. He therefore had no problem giving up to Saul all he knew about David and his conversation with Ahimelech. His warped mind earned him a place in this book.

4. 4. He knew how to instigate wickedness. 1 Samuel 22: 9-10 Doeg knew what the reaction of Saul would be. He instigated murder by giving Saul the information in such a way that would hurt and create a desire for revenge on the priests.

What can we in the 21st Century learn from Doeg?

A. By their works they shall be known! The very first time Doeg was introduced to us we find him detained before the LORD! The words "detained before the LORD" meant that he was probably there praying, seeking GOD, making the appropriate sacrifices and having a religious appearance, but inside him was murder, greed and every other kind of wickedness imaginable or unimaginable to the normal human mind.

Doeg is that type of person who professes to be a Christian, attends Church every Sunday, but lives however he wants. In a nutshell, change has failed to take place where it is needed the most: within the heart.

From Doeg we learn that GOD looks at the heart not the outward appearances of what a Christian should be. GOD is more interested in the fruits than the words people profess.

JESUS says, by their fruit they shall be known (**Matthew 7: 16**); NOT by their words. Another Scripture in the book of **Matthew, chapter 15: 19-20**, reminds us the heart is unclean because of the thoughts that dominate it.

Beware of wolves in sheep's clothing; not everyone who says they are Christians are true Christians, and definitely not everyone who comes to Church is saved, either. But by their works they shall be known. Keep your eyes open!

B. Greed is a killer disease. James chapter 4: 1-3 depicts what happens when people are greedy and covetous. One of the major

4

reasons Doeg chose to tell Saul about David was to have favour with him and get more things from Saul. He would put GOD's chosen king in danger and murder a family of priests just to acquire more material possessions. JESUS says that a man's life does not consist of the abundance of what he has (Luke 12: 15). In the same way we can learn from Doeg never to get carried away by the desire to acquire properties, cars, clothes and other things. As good and necessary as those things are, our affection must first be set on loving GOD, otherwise we could find ourselves doing the unimaginable just to get things.

C. Be on GOD's side. Remember, it was common knowledge in the land of Israel that David was the person GOD had chosen as king and Saul, outside of GOD's will, though he was still ruling **2 Samuel 19: 9:**" *9 Throughout the tribes of Israel, the people were all arguing with each other, saying, "The king delivered us from the hand of our enemies; he is the one who rescued us from the hand of the Philistines..."*

Also, the Bible tells us that David knew Doeg **1 Samuel 22: 22** and, of course, would have known the call on David's life. Even with such facts staring at him in the face, Doeg chose to align with Saul. We should always choose to align ourselves with GOD's chosen people as opposed to those he has rejected. Even when the association costs, GOD's chosen people have a grace to cover us in times of trouble as Abiathar found out when he ran to David.

Chapter Two: Abimelech

Scripture – Judges 9

Abimelech ranks as one of the top most wicked men in the Bible. Interestingly, fifty-two verses are used to chronicle his life in **Chapter 9** of the **Book of the Judges**, which is the longest chapter in the book!

Who is Abimelech?

He was the son of Jeru-Baal. Who is he? That is the other name for Gideon. Remember him? The one who put out fleece to test GOD who still answered his request since, at that time, the HOLY SPIRIT had not been sent like we have Him today.

Putting out fleece would not be the right way for a believer to hear from GOD. JESUS did not put out fleece; neither did Paul, Philip, Niconar, Stephen, or Priscilla!

Gideon did a lot of good by delivering the Children of Israel from the hands of the Midianites who brutally oppressed them.

However, towards the end of his life, he created an ephod which then became an instrument of worship for the Israelites. More than that, Gideon was also very active in the reproduction department, fathering seventy-five sons, one of whom was Abimelech, the son of one of his slave girls!

Judges 8: 29-31: *"Jerub-Baal son of Joash went back home to live. 30 He had seventy sons of his own, for he had many wives. 31 His concubine, who lived in Shechem, also bore him a son, whom he named Abimelech."*

7

Abimelech was reluctant to share rulership of the land when his father died. Instead, his life became a concoction of cold-blooded murder, deception and brutality of the kind Hollywood producers may struggle to put together, let alone find such occurrences in the Bible!

Abimelech's actions were more wicked than some of the "Godfathers" depicted in Hollywood films.

GOD had to get involved for his actions to be curtailed as we read in **Judges 9: 22-24:** " *After Abimelech had governed Israel three years, 23 God sent an evil spirit between Abimelech and the citizens of Shechem, who acted treacherously against Abimelech. 24 God did this in order that the crime against Jerub-Baal's seventy sons, the shedding of their blood, might be avenged on their brother Abimelech and on the citizens of Shechem, who had helped him murder his brothers. "*

What made Abimelech one of the most infamous?

1. **He killed 70 of his own brothers in one day! Judges 9: 5:** *"He went to his father's home in Ophrah and on one stone murdered his seventy brothers, the sons of Jerub-Baal. But Jotham, the youngest son of Jerub-Baal, escaped by hiding."*Thank GOD Jotham escaped the massacre and then placed a curse on him that came to pass not too long after the murders! Think about that, seventy men were slaughtered on one stone; the amount of human blood that would be poured out would have being inconceivable, yet you have no record of Abimelech recoiling at the sight of such devastation.

2. **He wanted to be king at any cost - Judges 9: 1-2 & 4-6:** *" Abimelech son of Jerub-Baal went to his mother's brothers in Shechem and said to them and to all his mother's clan, 2" Ask all the citizens of Shechem, 'Which is better for you: to have all seventy of Jerub-Baal's sons rule over you, or just one man?' Remember, I am your flesh and blood." 3When the brothers repeated all this to*

8

the citizens of Shechem, they were inclined to follow Abimelech, for they said, "He is our brother." 4 They gave him seventy shekels of silver from the temple of Baal-Berith, and Abimelech used it to hire reckless adventurers, who became his followers... 6 Then all the citizens of Shechem and Beth Millo gathered beside the great tree at the pillar in Shechem to crown Abimelech king."

3. **Abimelech took advantage of the current state of affairs**. With his father dead and his body still warm in the grave he made a plan that would put him on the throne by force. He gained the upper hand by inciting racial and tribal differentiation. Going to his mother's family and asking them in no uncertain terms to support his desire to be king. Interestingly, we are not aware how far he was in the linage but, being the son of a slave, he did not carry as much weight as those who were born of the married wives. Perhaps the people of Shechem thought that would put them in a privileged position but, as the story unfolds, Abimelech ended up killing all the people in that town of Shechem to fulfil the curse placed on them by Jotham.

4. **He burned 1000 men and women alive! Judges 9: 47-49:** *" When Abimelech heard that they had assembled there, 48 he and all his men went up Mount Zalmon. He took an ax and cut off some branches, which he lifted to his shoulders. He ordered the men with him, "Quick! Do what you have seen me do!" 49 So all the men cut branches and followed Abimelech. They piled them against the stronghold and set it on fire over the people inside. So all the people in the tower of Shechem, about a thousand men and women, also died. "* By this time the town of Shechem was split and some were inclined to follow Gaal and his brother who boasted they could get rid of Abimelech. However, the battle did not go their way and they were defeated by Abimelech and his men. When Abimelech returned to Shechem he went on a murderous rampage to pay the Shechmites for trying to

defect. When they got scared and hid in a tower, Abimelech knew just what to do. He burned them all alive. Here is an interesting fact: Although the Bible does not record the number of children killed in the massacre, there were probably hundreds, if not thousands, of children also killed. Remember that when the record of the feeding of the five thousand is mentioned in the Gospels (**Mark 6: 32-44 & John 6: 10**), it only recorded the men. But who would leave their children outside and go into a safe place? We can only assume that Abimelech also murdered all those innocent children indiscriminately!

5. **He was unrepentant - Judges 9: 16-20:** *"Now if you have acted honorably and in good faith when you made Abimelech king,   and if you have been fair to Jerub-Baal and his family, and if you have treated him as he deserves— 17 and to think that my father   fought for you, risked his life to rescue you from the hand of Midian 18(but today you have revolted against my father's family,   murdered his seventy sons on a single stone, and made Abimelech, the son of his slave girl, king over the citizens of Shechem because he is your brother)— 19 if then you have acted honorably and in good faith toward Jerub-Baal and his family today, may Abibe your joy, and may you be his, too! 20 But if you have not, let fire come out from Abimelech and consume you, citizens of Shechem and Beth Millo, and let fire come out from you, citizens of Shechem and Beth Millo, and consume Abimelech!"*Despite the overwhelming evidence staring him in the face, Abimelech (like Doeg) did not even bat an eyelid. His conscience was seared as with a hot iron; see **1 Timothy 4: 2**. If Jotham had stayed around, he would have been killed for even daring to bring the truth to Abimelech. As a matter of fact, he was so possessed by evil that only death could put a halt to his uncontrollable murderous actions.

What can we in the 21st Century learn from Abimelech?

A. Insight into the ills of polygamy Judges 8: 30 "He had seventy sons of his own, for he had many wives." Those who think they can have many children just because they can afford it financially should reconsider their position. In reality, once the death of the father occurs, it inevitably gives rise to sibling rivalry and all sorts of evil. Equally ridiculous are those who have children outside of wedlock by other or numerous women. They may think that too doesn't matter because the wife at home is not aware and that makes it okay. The long-term consequences can also be disastrous. For all the good that David did, having many wives was one of his areas of failure. As a matter of fact, Solomon saw that example and took it to inconceivable heights by marrying seven hundred women and having three hundred concubines.

B. The consequences of reckless ambition. Sometimes even "Born Again" tongue-talking Christians can fall foul of this. They go after jobs, cars, holidays, houses, clothes as though their lives depended on it. It is easy for us to condemn Abimelech because (thank GOD most of us will never commit murder) his sins are much more obvious.

But how many people do we hurt along the way because we want a promotion or a job? Perhaps Abimelech did not think he would descend to such evil, but it never starts big; always small. When Judas began to steal form the purse of our LORD he also never thought he could ever betray JESUS for money.

However, that action was the entry the devil needed to get himself involved in Judas's mind. **Ephesians 4: 27** commands us not to give a foothold to the devil. Let us remember the words of Paul that admonish us that it is a little yeast that works through the whole batch of dough (**1 Corinthians 5: 6**). Here is another Scripture to remember: **Luke 12: 15:** *"Then he said to them, "Watch out! Be on your guard against all kinds of greed; a man's life does not consist in the abundance of his possessions."*

11

C. Tribalistic Christianity – Judges 9: 3-4: "When the brothers repeated all this to the citizens of Shechem, they were inclined to follow Abimelech, for they said, "He is our brother." 4 They gave him seventy shekels of silver from the temple of Baal-Berith, and Abimelech used it to hire reckless adventurers, who became his followers." It is obvious that one of the reasons the Shechmites followed Abimelech was because he was their brother by place of birth. That means that despite the fact he was not suitable to be a leader they were willing to make him "Lord" over them just because his mother was from their town. This reminds me of what happened in **Acts 6: 1-2** where those serving food discriminated against the Grecian Jews: "*In those days when the number of disciples was increasing, the Grecian Jews among them complained against the Hebraic Jews because their widows were being overlooked in the daily distribution of food. 2 So the Twelve gathered all the disciples together and said, "It would not be right for us to neglect the ministry of the word of God in order to wait on tables"*.

Those men or women serving at the time were dishing out better quantities of food to those who belonged to their tribe and left other widows to suffer. The solution was very simple.

Get those who are led by the SPIRIT to do the work. The only way to combat racism, tribalism and every other evil is to walk by the SPIRIT. This is an area in which we as Christians still need to grow. I noticed that the issue of **Acts 6: 1-2** is still in the hearts of some of my brothers and sisters!

12

Chapter Three: Ziba

Scripture – 2 Samuel 9, 16 & 19

Ziba's story is that of greed and betrayal with actions spread across three chapters of the book of 2 Samuel. He is one of those characters you might not hear preached about most Sundays, but you will discover shortly why he enters this book; apart from the fact that my wife suggested him!

Who is Ziba?

After David became king over Hebron and Israel, he sought to make good his promise to Jonathan by having anyone alive from the family of Saul sit at his table. Through his enquiries a man named Ziba, who was a servant in the house of Saul, showed up to disclose to the king that a son of Jonathan called Mephibosheth was alive and well, though crippled in both legs. **Second Samuel 9:2-4:** *"²Now there was a servant of Saul's household named Ziba. They called him to appear before David, and the king said to him, "Are you Ziba?" "Your servant," he replied. ³ The king asked, "Is there no one still left of the house of Saul to whom I can show God's kindness?" Ziba answered the king, "There is still a son of Jonathan; he is crippled in both feet." ⁴"Where is he?" the king asked. Ziba answered, "He is at the house of Makir son of Ammiel in Lo Debar."*

Mephibosheth was brought from Lo Debar and given the right to sit and eat at the king's table; moreover, David restored to him the land and fields that belonged to Saul and required Ziba the servant to farm the land and give the proceeds to Mephibosheth. **2 Samuel 9:9-10:** *" Then the king summoned Ziba, Saul's servant, and said to him, "I have given your master's grandson*

everything that belonged to Saul and his family. ¹⁰ You and your
sons and your servants are to farm the land for him and bring in
the crops, so that your master's grandson may be provided for.
And Mephibosheth, grandson of your master, will always eat at
my table." (Now Ziba had fifteen sons and twenty servants)."

In this short passage we learn a little about Ziba. He had fifteen
sons and twenty servants. He was no ordinary servant, but a
wealthy one who served in the royal house. He reminds me of a
Chief Servant to the Royal Family or some rich Sheik in Saudi
Arabia! We are now at the season when Absalom, son of David,
had stolen the hearts of the Israelites away after returning from
exile since killing his brother Amnon who raped his sister
Tamar.

David had no choice but to flee the palace to avoid his own son
killing him. It was on this journey that Ziba thought it right to
connive and manoeuvre his way to greater success by betraying
his master, Mephibosheth.

What made Ziba one of the most infamous?

To get a good understanding of why Ziba has entered into the
list of the seven most Infamous men in the Bible, we must
follow the sequence of his actions. Although we do not find Ziba
killing anyone in these passages, his action could have led to the
king killing an innocent person, cause regret, and break a
covenant. This is just as good as killing and, in some sense, even
worse. Let us see.

1. **He presented a good front to David** When David was
   on the run, he pretended to be concerned by bringing
   food and wine for him. **Second Samuel 16:1-2:"** *When*
   David had gone a short distance beyond the summit,
   there was Ziba, the steward of Mephibosheth, waiting to
   meet him. He had a string of donkeys saddled and loaded

with two hundred loaves of bread, a hundred cakes of raisins, a hundred cakes of figs and a skin of wine." Nothing about that seems bad until you understand the answer he gave after the next question David asks in vs. 3, "..."*Where is your master's grandson?" Ziba said to him, "He is staying in Jerusalem, because he thinks, 'Today the house of Israel will give me back my grandfather's kingdom.'"* The true reason why Ziba gave the food was now revealed: he did this to present a good front to David, though discrediting his boss.

2. **Ziba portrayed his master Mephibosheth as a betrayer 2 Samuel 16:3:** *"The king then asked, "Where is your master's grandson?" Ziba said to him, "He is staying in Jerusalem, because he thinks, 'Today the house of Israel will give me back my grandfather's kingdom.'"* This single statement could have gotten Mephibosheth killed instantly. Ziba had presented him as a backstabbing ungrateful so and so that deserved nothing than death, since he was still harbouring envy and jealousy after all David had done for him. If you have a servant like Ziba you really do not need enemies!

3. **Ziba received material wealth in a cunning manner** - When we get to the heart of the matter, the true reason Ziba betrayed his boss comes to light in **2 Samuel 16:4:** *"Then the king said to Ziba, "All that belonged to Mephibosheth is now yours." "I humbly bow," Ziba said. "May I find favor in your eyes, my lord the king."* King David chose to spare Mephibosheth's life, but punished him by depriving him of some of the wealth or financial security that was in store for the crippled man and his family. Ziba could not have cared less! He was now considerably richer just by telling a ten-second lie.

4. **Ziba betrayed the trust given him by Mephibosheth** The truth is revealed in **2 Samuel 19:26-30:** *"He said, "My lord the king, since I your servant am lame, I said, 'I will have my donkey saddled and will ride on it, so I can go with the king.' But Ziba my servant betrayed me. 27 And he has slandered your servant to my lord the king.*

15

My lord the king is like an angel of God; so do whatever pleases you. ²⁸All my grandfather's descendants deserved nothing but death from my lord the king, but you gave your servant a place among those who eat at your table. So what right do I have to make any more appeals to the king?" ²⁹ The king said to him, "Why say more? I order you and Ziba to divide the fields." ³⁰ Mephibosheth said to the king, "Let him take everything, now that my lord the king has arrived home safely."

Mephibosheth had a chance to redeem himself by explaining the matter to the king. Although David rightly accepted his story he couldn't recall the words he had uttered, but asked both the servant (Ziba) and master (Mephibosheth) to share the goods. Mephibosheth, in humility and adoration for the king, wanted nothing but the king's safety. Here we see the evil in Ziba. He walked happily away with the booty!

What can we in the 21st Century learn from Ziba?

A. Be careful who you trust When you are in a dire situation, do not trust everyone except those who have been tried and tested. Ziba was not tested. As time went on we find that Ziba was not an honest person, but a betrayer! Mephibosheth was crippled in both feet and had to rely on others for transport. If we are in a position of need either for transport or a job or some money, use discernment before you ask for help.

B. Rash decisions can be dangerous As we look at David's actions, we cannot help but consider that he made a rash judgement by asking Ziba to keep the goods without verifying his story or hearing from Mephibosheth. We learn in **1 Corinthians 10:11:** *"These things happened to them as examples and were written down as warnings for us, on whom the fulfilment of the ages has come. ¹²So, if you think you are standing firm, be careful that you don't fall!"* I could just have seen myself making the same mistake as David did in the heat of the moment and in anger towards someone. The devil is out to throw spanners in the works of our relationships. Let us not be ignorant of the devil's schemes.

C. The importance of honouring commitment - This whole story of Ziba would never have come to light and the lessons learned would have been missed if David did not choose to honour the relationship and commitment he had with his friend Jonathan. Sometimes after a period of long absence of a friend, we very easily neglect or forget the commitment we have made with them. Just as David honoured his commitment to Jonathan and the generations that followed him, let us honour those commitments we have made even when it costs us.

Hence we should take the admonition of **Proverbs 29:20:** "*Do you see a man who speaks in haste? There is more hope for a fool than for him.*" Also **Ecclesiastes 5:2-3:** "*Do not be quick with your mouth, do not be hasty in your heart to utter anything before God. God is in heaven and you are on earth, so let your words be few. ³ As a dream comes when there are many cares, so the speech of a fool when there are many words.*" The point I am making here is that we should think carefully before we make any commitments because we need to honour them once made!

Chapter Four: Achan

Scripture – Joshua 7

Achan's beginning and end is chronicled in the whole of chapter 7 of the book of Joshua. His actions nearly stopped the will of GOD for Israel from taking place. As we will learn, his greed and covetousness caused the defeat of a whole nation.

Who is Achan?

Israel under the leadership of Joshua had just enjoyed a major success in the conquest of Jericho after walking around it thirteen times and seeing the walls collapse! One of the most interesting parts of this miraculous event is that Jericho was the pathway to all the other cities GOD had given to Israel and the defeat of this major city sent the fear of the Children of Israel into the hearts of all the other nations.

It was shortly after this success that Joshua sent spies to Ai, the next city on their list of conquests. When the spies returned they advised that only three thousand men were necessary to take the city. Those three thousand were sent but were defeated with thirty-six Israelites soldiers dead! This was a shock to Israel and caused nationwide mourning, with Joshua flat on his face before GOD.

It was here the story of Achan begins; GOD told Joshua the reason for defeat in **Joshua 7:11-13:** *"Israel has sinned; they have violated my covenant, which I commanded them to keep. They have taken some of the devoted things; they have stolen, they have lied, they have put them with their own possessions. 12 That is why the Israelites cannot stand against their enemies; they turn their backs and run because they have been made* *liable to destruction. I will not be with you anymore unless you destroy whatever among you is devoted to destruction* [13] *"Go, consecrate the people. Tell them, 'Consecrate yourselves in preparation for tomorrow; for this is what the Lord, the God of Israel, says: That which is devoted is among you, O Israel. You cannot stand against your enemies until you remove it."*

As you read, you discover one of the most shocking truths of the Scriptures: the sin of Achan was concluded by GOD to be the sin of the whole nation of Israel! Due to the actions of Achan, Israel would always be defeated in battle. Read the chapter, please! As the LORD instructed, the filtering process started firstly tribe by tribe, then clan by clan, and then family by family. Achan's sin was revealed at the end of the process and he finally admitted his sin before being sent to his death by stoning. This act is taken in **Joshua 7:16-18 & 25:** "[16] *Early the next morning Joshua had Israel come forward by tribes, and Judah was taken.* [17] *The clans of Judah came forward, and he took the Zerahites. He had the clan of the Zerahites come forward by families, and Zimri was taken.* [18] *Joshua had his family come forward man by man, and Achan son of Carmi, the son of Zimri, the son of Zerah, of the tribe of Judah, was taken...* [25] *Joshua said, "Why have you brought this trouble on us? The Lord will bring trouble on you today." Then all Israel stoned him, and after they had stoned the rest, they burned them."*

What made Achan one of the most infamous?

Achan's story at the onset seemed like a small issue but, when you consider the consequences of his actions, he deserves to be amongst the seven most infamous Bad Boys. We find that he disobeyed GOD by taking some of the devoted things. "Devoted things" are those possessions that must be completely destroyed as ordered by GOD. Later on, Saul, when told to completely destroy the Amalekites in the book of Samuel, followed the same disobedience and that cost him his kingship.

Here are more five reasons why Achan's story is in this book.

1. **Achan caused the defeat of the nation of Israel Joshua 7:20-21:** *"[20]Achan replied, "It is true! I have sinned against the Lord, the God of Israel. This is what I have done: [21]When I saw in the plunder a beautiful robe from Babylonia, two hundred shekels of silver and a wedge of gold weighing fifty shekels, I coveted them and took them. They are hidden in the ground inside my tent, with the silver underneath."* The defeat of the children of Israel was such a surprise that they began to wonder whether GOD had departed from them, not knowing that Achan was the source of the nation's trouble.

2. **He had an unrepentant heart** Achan did not come forward, knowing that he had sinned. He tried to hide his actions but was found out by GOD's process of selection. We can conclude that he did not know what is later explained in the Scripture, **Proverbs 28:13:** *"He who conceals his sins does not prosper, but whoever confesses and renounces them finds mercy.*

3. **His actions brought death to his family Joshua 7:24:** *"Then Joshua, together with all Israel, took Achan son of Zerah, the silver, the robe, the gold wedge, his sons and daughters, his cattle, donkeys and sheep, his tent and all that he had, to the Valley of Achor."* Achan brought death to his family. Not only was he found guilty; his hands were filled with the blood of his sons, daughters, and even his possessions were considered corrupted.

4. **At least forty-one people died on account of him** If you count the thirty-six killed in battle plus the average size of a Jewish family then.

5. **His actions could have halted GOD's plan for Israel and emboldened their enemies, Joshua 7:8-9:** *"O Lord, what can I say, now that Israel has been routed by its enemies? [9] The Canaanites and the other people of the country will hear about this and they will surround us*

21

and wipe out our name from the earth. What then will you do for your own great name?" If the other nations had heard they were defeated by such a small city they would have been filled with courage and made the conquest of their own nation much harder. Not only that, such a defeat would have affected the army of Israel adversely. Achan was responsible for this emotional upheaval within the Israelites camp

What can we in the 21st Century learn from Achan?

A. One man's sin can affect a nation Your sin affects your nation. There is a prevailing thought in the Western part of the world that is extremely unbiblical. It is the idea of living as you like; that your actions are purely for yourself. That is what Achan thought too. He felt that disobeying GOD and taking some of the devoted things would not hurt anyone. How wrong he was.

Let me give you an example closer to home. Those who have children out of wedlock may consider themselves to have been two consenting adults and that their actions only affected them alone. However, you and I know that is simply not the case. Crimes are largely committed by children from single parent homes. Also, having been a Youth Pastor for five years, I witnessed the stark difference in the mental state of those from a single parent home and those who came from a home with married parents (male and female).

We are told in **1 Corinthians 12:12-13 & 25-26** that we are all one body: *"12 The body is a unit, though it is made up of many parts; and though all its parts are many, they form one body. So it is with Christ. 13 For we were all baptized by one Spirit into one body— whether Jews or Greeks, slave or free—and we were all given the one Spirit to drink... 25 so that there should be no division in the body, but that its parts should have equal concern for each other. 26 If one part suffers, every part suffers with it; if* *one part is honored, every part rejoices with it."*

Remember Galatians chapter two Paul spoke up against Apostle Peter's action? He made a remarkable statement that his actions even led Barnabas astray. **Galatians 2:12-13:** *"12 Before certain men came from James, he used to eat with the Gentiles. But when they arrived, he began to draw back and separate himself from the Gentiles because he was afraid of those who belonged to the circumcision group. 13 The other Jews joined him in his hypocrisy, so that by their hypocrisy even Barnabas was led astray."*

I am sure Adam thought his sin only affected him too, but how wrong was he? **Romans 5:12:** *"Therefore, just as sin entered the world through one man, and death through sin, and in this way death came to all men, because all sinned—"*Your actions, my actions, affect the whole body!

B. Disobedience still has consequences for your family We see in this story that Achan's family were also stoned to death. Today, when we fail to follow GOD's instructions though HE forgives us and will always forgive us, we may still suffer the consequence of the sin. Moreover, that consequence may affect our families. In **Ephesians 4:27** Paul tells the church that those who have been stealing must stop and must do something with their hands. If any choose to disobey that and continue to steal; if is the persons are caught though they will be forgiven if they repent, their actions will lead them to jail and the family will suffer loss and humiliation.

C. Sin costs more than if things had been done the right way at the outset – Joshua 8:1-2: *"Then the Lord said to Joshua, "Do not be afraid; do not be discouraged. Take the whole army with you, and go up and attack Ai. For I have delivered into your hands the king of Ai, his people, his city and his land. 2 You shall do to Ai and its king as you did to Jericho and its king, except that you may carry off their plunder and livestock for yourselves.*

Set an ambush behind the city." By the time you read about the taking of Ai the whole Israelite army was needed for the conquest that should have been done by three thousand people. Here is the lesson for you and me in the twenty-first century. when we sin, more effort is required from us to get back to the same place GOD wants us to be. This is the reason why many who sin stay in the same condition—because they have not realised this truth.

Let us consider what we do and, if we think our actions are opposed to GOD's will, withdraw from them so that our family, Church, and our nation will not be affected.

Chapter Five: Judas Iscariot

Scripture - Luke 6:12-16!

Now for a New Testament Bad Boy who betrayed our LORD and SAVIOUR JESUS CHRIST.

Who is Judas?

Exactly when Judas became a Disciple we are not told; unlike the history of Peter's call or Nathaniel's encounter with the LORD in **John chapter 1**. What we do know is that Judas was not just a Disciple of JESUS; he was also an Apostle. This means that he started walking with the LORD very early in His ministry, which tells us that, apart from the miracles He did privately while with Peter, James, and John, all others were witnessed by Judas. For example, he was there in the book of Luke when the lepers were cleansed and one came back praising GOD. He was there during the feeding of the five thousand and when JESUS healed the paralytic, as well as many other miracles recorded in the book of Luke alone! He heard JESUS'S sermons, parables, teachings and instructions first hand!

Apart from all these, Judas himself performed many miracles **Apart from all these, Judas himself performed many miracles &:** *"...and Judas Iscariot, who betrayed him.[5] These twelve Jesus sent out with the following instructions: "Do not go among the Gentiles or enter any town of the Samaritans. [6]Go rather to the lost sheep of Israel. [7]As you go, preach this message: 'The kingdom of heaven is near.' [8]Heal the sick, raise the dead, cleanse those who have leprosy, drive out demons. Freely you have received, freely give."*

25

He also had the trusted position of looking after the funds of JESUS (for those who think JESUS did not have access to any money, I wonder how they deal with the Scripture that tell us HE had a treasurer!) Judas was accustomed to being sent to carry out certain expenditures or to disburse the purse, **John 13:29:** *"Since Judas had charge of the money, some thought Jesus was telling him to buy what was needed for the Feast, or to give something to the poor."* This alone meant he had regular contact with JESUS as in the case of a Business Owner speaking with his Finance Director.

But Judas had a dark side. He must have had regular contact with the Chief Priest and Pharisees who wanted JESUS dead; **Luke 22:4-6:** *"4 And Judas went to the chief priests and the officers of the temple guard and discussed with them how he might betray Jesus. 5They were delighted and agreed to give him money. 6He consented, and watched for an opportunity to hand Jesus over to them when no crowd was present."*

He was also a thief; we get this truth from the account of **John 13:4-6:** *"4But one of his disciples, Judas Iscariot, who was later to betray him, objected, 5"Why wasn't this perfume sold and the money given to the poor? It was worth a year's wages." 6He did not say this because he cared about the poor but because he was a thief; as keeper of the money bag, he used to help himself to what was put into it."* He was a thief and his love for money got him to commit one of the most serious crimes ever. This is what JESUS had to say about the one who betrays Him: **Matthew 26:24:** *"The Son of Man will go just as it is written about him. But woe to that man who betrays the Son of Man! It would be better for him if he had not been born."*

The suggestion has always been made that JESUS knew who would betray Him even before the earth was formed, to which I agree and say, yes! Scriptures say that one close to Him would betray Him; this I also agree with. However, I would say, though it was Judas, it did not have to be Judas. His own heart led him into this sin for which he paid dearly!

What made Judas one of the most infamous?

1. **He betrayed the Author of Salvation** According to thefreedictionary.com, "betray" means: a. To give aid or information to an enemy of; commit treason against: betray one's country; b. To deliver into the hands of an enemy in violation of a trust or allegiance. Judas had no issue delivering JESUS into the hands of his enemies. As a matter of fact, at the garden of Gethsemane, JESUS asked Judas this question in **Luke 22:47-48:** *"⁴⁷While he was still speaking a crowd came up, and the man who was called Judas, one of the Twelve, was leading them. He approached Jesus to kiss him, ⁴⁸but Jesus asked him, "Judas, are you betraying the Son of Man with a kiss?"*

2. **He sided with the enemies of JESUS** He had seen the way JEUS lived, heard the things He said and followed Him around for three years, but sided with the Jewish rulers who decided that JESUS deserved to die; **Luke 22:1-3:** *"Now the Feast of Unleavened Bread, called the Passover, was approaching, ²and the chief priests and the teachers of the law were looking for some way to get rid of Jesus, for they were afraid of the people. ³Then Satan entered Judas, called Iscariot, one of the Twelve."*

3. **Judas put the lives of his bosom friends at risk** Judas lived with the other apostles for the period in which he was with JESUS. When Judas therefore brought the soldiers to arrest JESUS there was nothing stopping them from arresting and crucifying the other apostles. These men were Judas's friends. Hence, JESUS pleaded for their lives in **John 18:8-9:** *"I told you that I am he,"* *Jesus answered. "If you are looking for me, then let these men go." ⁹This happened so that the words he had spoken would be fulfilled: "I have not lost one of those*

you gave me." As a matter of fact, the apostles were still frightened after the death of CHRIST, as the Scripture tells us in **John 20:19:** *" On the evening of that first day of the week, when the disciples were together, with the doors locked for fear of the Jews, Jesus came and stood among them and said, "Peace be with you!"* It is for the fear of life (among other reasons) Peter even denied the LORD. Judas's actions put his own friends in a vulnerable position!

What can we in the 21st Century learn from Judas?

A. The faithfulness of GOD JESUS knew that Judas would betray Him, yet He still gave him all the chances he needed to make a change.

In the same way, when we receive JESUS, He gives us the HOLY SPIRIT—**2 Corinthians 2:21-22:** *"Now it is God who makes both us and you stand firm in Christ. He anointed us, 22set his seal of ownership on us, and put his Spirit in our hearts as a deposit, guaranteeing what is to come."* GOD continues to work in us according to **Philippians 2:13:** *"For it is God who works in you to will and to act according to his good purpose."* and prunes us according to **John 15:2** so that we can keep on bearing fruit! *"He cuts off every branch in me that bears no fruit, while every branch that does bear fruit he prunes so that it will be even more fruitful."*

Our GOD is a good GOD. Judas had all the chances in the world to do the right thing; he chose not to.

B . We must finish well Judas was in Church, performed miracles with the other apostles, was mightily used by GOD, but did not finish well. Our salvation is about finishing well. One can be in Church and still not make it to the end. Paul said in **2 Timothy 4:7-8:** *"7I have fought the good fight, I have finished the race, I have kept the faith. 8Now there is in store for me the*

28

crown of righteousness, which the Lord, the righteous Judge, will award to me on that day—and not only to me, but also to all who have longed for his appearing."

Colossians 1:22-23: *"²²But now he has reconciled you by Christ's physical body through death to present you holy in his sight, without blemish and free from accusation— ²³if you continue in your faith, established and firm, not moved from the hope held out in the gospel."* **Hebrews 10:36-39:** *"³⁶You need to persevere so that when you have done the will of God, you will receive what he has promised. ³⁷For in just a very little while, "He who is coming will come and will not delay. ³⁸But my righteous one will live by faith. And if he shrinks back, I will not be pleased with him." ³⁹But we are not of those who shrink back and are destroyed, but of those who believe and are saved."*

C. We need to know GOD It is my personal belief that there were times when Judas could have repented and saved himself from eternal damnation but he did not yield. Think about Peter's denial. That was a big thing too, but he repented and was restored three times for the denials in **John 21**. Our knowledge of GOD should always bring us to repentance, not drive us to suicide. Judas took his own life instead of receiving and embracing the love of the LORD. Peter chose to face the LORD and was restored. You and I should repent and face the LORD if we sin, for He has and will forgive us (this is not a license to sin) because we know we are HIS Children.

Chapter Six: Baanah and Recab

Scripture – 2 Samuel 4

"Hold on!" I hear you say. "There are seven chapters and we have two people in the sixth!" The last two chapters include duos whom I have considered as one because they are related. Now that we've cleared that up, let's continue!

If little is known of Doeg the Edomite by most, you might not have come across Baanah and his brother Recab, sons of Rimon the Beerothite of the tribe of Benjamin, either. However, you are about to be introduced to two of the worst people ever recorded in the Bible. Actually, King David called them wicked men that are not worthy to remain on the earth.

Who are these two men?

Let's step back in history. We are now at the stage when David was ruling in Hebron but not the whole of Israel as GOD planned, because Saul had just died in battle with some of his sons, including David's friend Jonathan. Remember that Saul's method of operation was to gather brave men around him and get them to do his work with the incentive of gifts of fields, vineyards and many other things he could use to pacify their souls. We find his son IshBosheth following the practice of choosing valiant men Baanah and Recah to lead his raiding bands.

Another piece of history that is relevant here is that Abner (Saul's commander), had just been killed by Joab (David's commander) who avenged the death of his brother Asahel whom Abner killed during the war between the houses of David and Saul (**2 Samuel 2**). Joab nursed a grudge and made sure he took revenge, but in peacetime. Ish-Bosheth, the son of Saul who was ruling at the time, was so frightened when Abner died, we are told in **2 Samuel 4:1** that *"When Ish-Bosheth son of Saul heard that Abner had died in Hebron, he lost courage, and all Israel became alarmed."*

So at this point Ish-Bosheth was no match, nor did he pose any kind of threat, to David. However, these two men thought they had a better plan of appealing to David and they went into Ish-Bosheth's house, entered his bedroom, stabbed him, cut off his head, and travelled all night with it to present it to David. David was far from impressed and concluded they needed to die instantly for such vile actions. The Bible records how they died in **2 Samuel 4:12**: *"So David gave an order to his men, and they killed them. They cut off their hands and feet and hung the bodies by the pool in Hebron. But they took the head of Ish-Bosheth and buried it in Abner's tomb at Hebron."* One small chapter of twelve verses is dedicated to the actions of these men, but the stench of their evil practice smells right through the centuries.

What made Baanah and Recab most infamous?

1. They killed a king in his own bed – 2 Samuel 4:9-11:
"As surely as the Lord lives, who has delivered me out of all trouble, ¹⁰when a man told me, 'Saul is dead,' and thought he was bringing good news, I seized him and put him to death in Ziklag. That was the reward I gave him for his news! ¹¹ How much more—when wicked men have killed an innocent man in his own house and on his own bed—should I not now demand his blood from your hand

and rid the earth of you!" One's house ought to be a palace of safety. As the saying goes, "an Englishman's house is his castle." These two men violated that principle, using their talents to enter his home and chop off his head.

2. **Ish-Bosheth was an innocent man 2 Samuel 4:11:** *"How much more— when wicked men have killed an innocent man in his own house and on his own bed— should I not now demand his blood from your hand and rid the earth of you!"* The reason David called him innocent was not because he was unaware that Saul's son was his enemy but because he knew that his trust was in Abner and when he was dead the war was over. Also, Ish-Bosheth was not coming to fight David because he was probably afraid of him. For that reason, he is declared to be innocent and the two brothers evil.

3. **They killed in peacetime** It is an acceptable fact that people die during a war. David was a fair man and would not accept such a killing in peacetime under any guise. Remember that David had many opportunities to kill Saul but did not use them; how much more if Ish-Bosheth is in his home, in bed away from any battlefield, would David not seek to protect him.

4. **They tried to spiritualise their act 2 Samuel 4:8:** *"They brought the head of Ish-Bosheth to David at Hebron and said to the king, "Here is the head of Ish-Bosheth son of Saul, your enemy, who tried to take your life. This day the Lord has avenged my lord the king against Saul and his offspring."* Many times wicked men try to use GOD as the one behind their actions. They had gone and killed an innocent man in his own bed and tried to pass off their actions as GOD's will. David was smart enough to see through their words and straight to their evil hearts as he recognised the absence of GOD in this case.They failed to realise that other men had tried to no avail to talk David into killing Saul while coating their words in spiritual language, but their persuasion just washed off him. He was not going to fall for it. Evil

people can use GOD's name all day long, but their fruits speak all day long too! When they use words like " *your enemy, who tried to take your life. This day the Lord has avenged my lord the king against Saul and his offspring,*" what they are really saying is "GOD told us to do it!""

5. **They betrayed the trust given them by Ish-Bosheth's household** Notice they went to his room under false pretences. **2 Samuel 4:6** says, *"They went into the inner part of the house as if to get some wheat, and they stabbed him in the stomach. Then Recab and his brother Baanah slipped away."* They could only have gotten past the guards because they were known in that house as men belonging to and loyal to Ish-Bosheth, otherwise they would have not gone past the fence. Evil people can violate the trust they have been given without even flinching. Here we find Baanah and Recab did just that!

6. **They knew where Ish-Bosheth would be sleeping 2 Samuel 2:5:** *"Now Recab and Baanah, the sons of Rimmon the Beerothite, set out for the house of Ish-Bosheth, and they arrived there in the heat of the day while he was taking his noonday rest."* Since they worked for him, they knew his routine. This reminds me of the betrayal of JESUS by Judas. Judas led the detachment of soldiers to the place JESUS frequently stayed and then kissed Him as a means of identifying Him to the soldiers. Such was the betrayal of Baanah and Recab, taking advantage of their inside knowledge to slay an innocent man for their own gain.

What can we in the 21ˢᵗ Century learn from Baanah and Recab?

A. People who do evil to gain your friendship will do the same to you Baanah and Recab wanted to gain friendship and loyalty to the king, and obviously desired to have high positions with him at the same time. David knew their actions were not right and, if they killed Ish-Bosheth who had trusted them, they would kill David just as easily when they became dissatisfied with him.

This reminds me of people who go to interviews and bad-mouth their previous employer. A smart prospective new employer will avoid employing them because they will do the same to them when they move on. New positions should never be attained at the expense of others!

B. Wait for GOD's promotion David had gone through so much and this incident again reinforces his commitment to GOD and their commitment to evil. David wanted to have the kingdom GOD's way. This chapter speaks about Baanah and Recab as well as David, whom we find at the centre of story. David wanted GOD to turn over the kingdom to him, not these two men. Here is the deal. If they gave David the kingdom, they would never let him forget that, and he never wanted to be in debt to evil. Who is the one putting us in positions GOD (using people), or people using any means necessary?

Psalm 75:6-7: "*6 For promotion cometh neither from the east, nor from the west, nor from the south. 7 But God is the judge: he putteth down one, and setteth up another.* We need to trust GOD to promote us and wait for His divine timing, and not try to get ahead on our own, for that is the devil's wish.

C. Instant removal - Although in the New Testament people did not kill like David did, we can still learn from the way he dealt with evil. David was quick to get rid of them and did it fast! **2 Samuel 4:11:** " *How much more—when wicked men have killed an innocent man in his own house and on his own bed— should I not now demand his blood from your hand and rid the earth of you!" 12 So David gave an order to his men, and they killed them. They cut off their hands and feet and hung the bodies by the pool in Hebron.*"

We must deal with evil decisively and make no provision for it. **Romans 13:14** *says, "But put ye on the Lord Jesus Christ, and* *make not provision for the flesh, to fulfil the lusts thereof."* **1 Peter 2:1:** *"Therefore, rid yourselves of all malice and all deceit, hypocrisy, envy, and slander of every kind. ²Like newborn babies, crave pure spiritual milk, so that by it you may grow up in your salvation, ³now that you have tasted that the Lord is good."*

We ought to strive to be in the position that CHRIST was when He said, "Satan comes but finds nothing in me!" (**John 14:30**).

Chapter Seven: Ananias and Sapphira

Scripture – Acts 5

Here are the husband and wife "Sinful Tag team" who appear in **Acts, chapter 5**! I hope you will permit me to use this couple as male entity for the sake of the book. For those needing scriptural backing, please see the words of JESUS in **Matthew 19:5-6**.

Who are Ananias and Sapphira?

The Church began its upward momentous growth from one hundred twenty members to three thousand in one day, plus many others being added daily. The new believer's actions were well cataloged by **Acts 2:42-47** which says: *"42 They devoted themselves to the apostles' teaching and to the fellowship, to the breaking of bread and to prayer. 43 Everyone was filled with awe, and many wonders and miraculous signs were done by the apostles. 44 All the believers were together and had everything in common. 45 Selling their possessions and goods, they gave to anyone as he had need. 46 Every day they continued to meet together in the temple courts. They broke bread in their homes and ate together with glad and sincere hearts, 47 praising God and enjoying the favor of all the people. And the Lord added to their number daily those who were being saved."*

From the above we get a complete sense of devotion to CHRIST, love to GOD and the Brethren, unity and power that we might even long for today. The apostles and other believers gained ground, won souls, and endured suffering to expand the Kingdom. We are then introduced to Barnabas, and the husband

and wife team of Ananias and Sapphira. The writer of the book, Dr. Luke, gives us the contrast: *"36 Joseph, a Levite from Cyprus, whom the apostles called Barnabas (which means Son of Encouragement), 37 sold a field he owned and brought the money and put it at the apostles' feet."*

Here we see a man who later became an apostle doing the right thing by contributing to the needs of the poor without any pretence. We are introduced to the sinful tag team who sold their property as well and then pretended as though they brought the whole proceeds to the Church. Exactly when did this couple come to faith? We are not told. Were they Believers? My answer would be, yes they were.

Peter saw through their lies and pretence. Since their responses were not fitting to the New Testament standards, their deception earned them the reward; death!

What made Ananias and Sapphira most infamous?

Although we do not find Ananias and Sapphira putting a knife to someone's throat, their actions could have had far reaching consequences if they were not dealt with. They put the growth of the church at risk, tried to hinder the flow of the Spirit and operated under the spiritual influence of the devil and not GOD!

1. **They were the first couple to be disciplined in church for lying** JESUS said in **John 8:43-44** that Satan is a liar and a father of lies: *"43 Why is my language not clear to you? Because you are unable to hear what I say. 44 You belong to your father, the devil, and you want to carry out your father's desire. He was a murderer from the beginning, not holding to the truth, for there is no truth in him. When he lies, he speaks his native language, for he is a liar and the father of lies."* Ananias and Sapphira chose to lie, thinking they could deceive the Church. Here is the real issue: if they were allowed to get away

38

with that lie it would have ruined the purity of the Church by causing other Believers to follow their example and the early Church's power would have been eroded!By the time you read **Acts 5 verses 12 and 15-16:** *"¹² The apostles performed many miraculous signs and wonders among the people. And all the believers used to meet together in Solomon's Colonnade... ¹⁵ As a result, people brought the sick into the streets and laid them on beds and mats so that at least Peter's shadow might fall on some of them as he passed by. ¹⁶ Crowds gathered also from the towns around Jerusalem, bringing their sick and those tormented by evil spirits, and all of them were healed."*You come to realise what could have happened if they were not dealt with.

2. **They coveted praise and honour without being prepared to earn it.** Ananias and Sapphira are in this book because they tried to copy what Barnabas did, but without his heart. Surely selling your land and bringing the proceeds to the Church was a big deal, as it would be now. I presume that the Church gave Barnabas the attention craved by Ananias and Sapphira. However, they chose to receive this accolade by deception, **Acts 5:1-2:** *"Now a man named Ananias, together with his wife Sapphira, also sold a piece of property. ²With his wife's full knowledge he kept back part of the money for himself, but brought the rest and put it at the apostles' feet."*

3. **Their act would have hindered the salvation of many** – **Acts 5:11-14:** *"¹¹ Great fear seized the whole church and all who heard about these events. ¹²The apostles performed many miraculous signs and wonders among the people. And all the believers used to meet together in Solomon's Colonnade. ¹³No one else dared join them, even though they were highly regarded by the people. ¹⁴ Nevertheless, more and more men and women believed in the Lord and were added to their number."* This great fear was probably what they never considered, but was

vital to the growth of the Church. What would have happened if they were allowed to keep up their evil intent? The unsaved would have considered the Church a joke and not bothered with salvation. But the opposite took place once they were dealt with: people got saved!

What can we in the 21st Century learn from Ananias and Sapphira?

Many of us might struggle with the decision of Peter's death sentence and perhaps we may feel that the harshness of this type of discipline is undeserved.

A. Though you are believer, Satan can fill your heart Rather than get involved in the debate over whether a Believer can be demon-possessed or not, it is worth considering what **Acts 5:3** teaches: *"Then Peter said, "Ananias, how is it that Satan has so filled your heart that you have lied to the Holy Spirit and have kept for yourself some of the money you received for the land?"* A Believer's heart can be filled with satanic thoughts. This happens when you open yourself up to Satan's ideals and fleshly desires.

Let us look at another example in **Matthew 16:17 & 22-23:** " *Jesus replied, "Blessed are you, Simon son of Jonah, for this was not revealed to you by man, but by my Father in heaven. 22 Peter took him aside and began to rebuke him. "Never, Lord!" he said. "This shall never happen to you!"...23 Jesus turned and said to Peter, "Get behind me, Satan! You are a stumbling block to me; you do not have in mind the things of God, but the things of men."*

Observe in one minute Peter was accurate in the Spirit; the next he is being used by the devil! Bible says in **Proverbs 4:24:** *"Above all else, guard your heart, for it is the wellspring of life."*

B. The power that exists within the Church Many may not

realise this, but the Church has power to exercise discipline. **1 Corinthians 5:4-5:** *"⁴ When you are assembled in the name of our Lord Jesus and I am with you in spirit, and the power of our Lord Jesus is present, ⁵ hand this man over to Satan, so that the sinful nature may be destroyed and his spirit saved on the day of the Lord."* **Another example of discipline is found in 1 Timothy 5:***20: "Those who sin are to be rebuked publicly, so that the others may take warning."* The Church ought to be careful about how this authority is used, as we all need to be aware that it is there for a purpose. On rare occasions where we perceive the approval of the HOLY SPIRIT, such authority must be exercised. I know that this really goes against the belief of many Christians.

C. **Don't join forces in telling lies – Acts 5:7-9:** *" About three hours later his wife came in, not knowing what had happened. ⁸ Peter asked her, "Tell me, is this the price you and Ananias got for the land?" "Yes," she said, "that is the price." ⁹ Peter said to her, "How could you agree to test the Spirit of the Lord? Look! The feet of the men who buried your husband are at the door, and they will carry you out also."* Now in this Scripture in **Acts 5,** interestingly, Peter gave Sapphira a chance to tell the truth but she chose to lie like her husband. Sapphira did not need to die if she had told the truth. Though husbands and wives are one, there is still the individual responsibility of telling the truth.

Is that what you and I do, or do we blindly follow our spouses?

Conclusion

All The Bad Boys & You

Before you condemn all the above "Bad Boys" in your heart or compare your secret/public sin to theirs, I want to remind you of a spiritual truth: as far as GOD is concerned, "All have sinned." And that word "All" includes you except you who have given your life to JESUS.

It includes those who say, "I will never murder anyone," "I don't use foul language or listen to sexually explicit music."

If you think along these lines, you are definitely within the "All" because you have trusted in your own self-righteousness! The big deal is, you have never been 100% sinless and, as such as far as spiritual laws are concerned, if you commit one sin you are as good as sinning all the way!

So here comes the good news: JESUS! Let me give you these two Bible verses to help: **2 Corinthians 5:21:** *21 God made him who had no sin to be sin[a] for us, so that in him we might become the righteousness of God.* The second is **Romans 3:23-24: There is no difference, 23for all have sinned and fall short of the glory of God, 24and are justified freely by his grace through the redemption that came by Christ Jesus.**

You see, JESUS declared that every evil act comes from the heart and the only reason that is so is because the heart of man is desperately wicked. However, when you give your life to JESUS, He then gives you a new heart, pronounces you holy and righteous, as well as gives you a new desire. You no longer have to rely on yourself but what He achieved for you on the cross.

You don't have to worry about your end because you have eternal salvation. You no long have to worry about being a "Bad Boy" because you would not desire to be bad. Why? Because when you submit your will to GOD, He will lead you by the HOLY SPIRIT.

If you want to give you life to JESUS you can start by saying this prayer:

FATHER I thank you for the provision you have made for me. I confess with my mouth that "JESUS is LORD"

and I believe in my heart that you raised him from the dead.

Right now I receive the salvation that comes through him and ask you to fill me with your SPIRIT. Thank you for forgiving me all my sins and making me holy and righteous.

If you meant this prayer when you said it, then you are Born Again. You need to find a Bible-believing Church to attend regularly and join their Discipleship program. If you need any help,

e-mail me: admin@boomytokanministries.com

Thank you so much for reading my book. I hope you really liked it.

As you probably know, many people look at the reviews on Amazon before they decide to purchase a book. If you liked the book, could you please take a minute to leave a review with your feedback?

60 seconds is all I'm asking for, and it would mean the world to me.

Thank you so much,

Boomy Tokan,

admin@boomytokanministries.com

T: +44 7932 394620

Other Books By Boomy Tokan

The Bad Girls Of The Bible - 7 Most Infamous

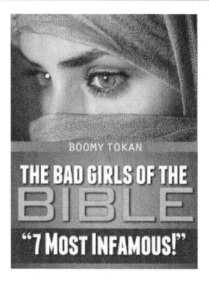

Ever wondered why some people are just – bad? In this book you will discover some well-known characters and other obscure ones that can teach you life lessons for the 21st Century. This book will educate and inspire you!

The Church Choir (Vol. 1): 10 Things Every Gospel Singer Must Know

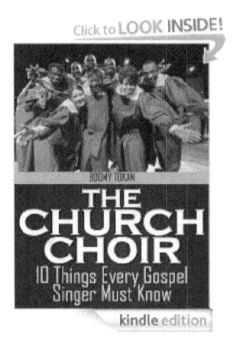

Church Choirs are one of the most important ministries in any 21st Century Church. They have the ability to affect the way a congregation worships; therefore it is vital that all members of a Choir are effectively functioning in a manner that pleases GOD. This book is a call to provide excellence in the area of worship leading by highlighting some of the aspects that are often missed or poorly executed. It should help any Church Choir to align itself to GOD's will, so that they can consistently deliver SPIRIT-filled worship!

__Church Choirs: 10 Habits of Highly Effective Choirs!__

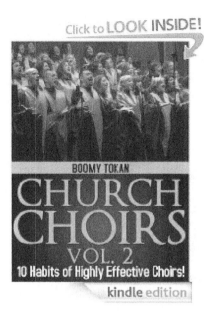

This is the Part 2 to *The Church Choir: 10 Things Every Gospel Singer Must Know*. In this book we take a look into the in-depth practices that make a choir successful (in the eyes of JESUS). Consideration is given to habits that will ensure the success of the group and the GOD-driven effects it can have on congregants. You will find it to be a useful guide if you are in a Church Choir and a good eye opener to better worship if you are a congregant!

Famous Bible Verses: 21 Most Misquoted Verses

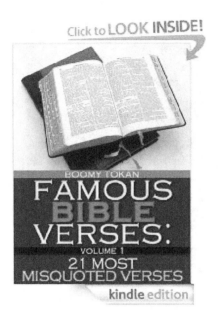

True knowledge of the Scriptures has to be based on accurate meaning, context and right application. This book, *21 Most Misquoted Verses*, will help you in your journey to true knowledge.

Noah's Ark - "What Happened To The Fish During Noah's Flood?!" (Famous Bible Verses)

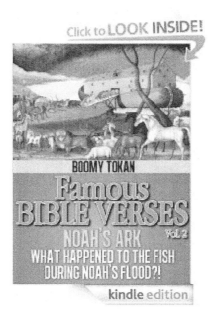

If you have never thought about this then you must join the thousands of believers who sit around the table to discuss such interesting Bible questions. Boomy Tokan gives 12 clear answers that will greatly help you to understand the facts surrounding this question.

How To Write Your First Business Plan: With Outline and Templates Book

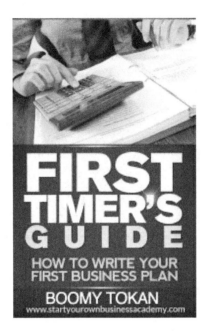

(Includes USA-friendly content, plus the principles taught in this book are transferable to any country.) Whenever the words "Business Plan" are mentioned, most people freeze! What follows are the words "I don't know how to write one."

In reality it need not be this way. That is why I have taken the lid off and written in plain English what needs to be considered and included within a business plan. This book has been written to help those who are writing plans for the first time or for those who write business plans infrequently. (Even seasoned business plan writers will learn one or two things, I promise!) Finally, I have included my personal email for those who need further assistance. This service will be offered FREE for now.

New Year's Resolutions: The Guide to Getting It Right Why Many New Year Resolutions Fail Within 30 Days How To Make Yours Work and Kick Start Your Year Book. (The Right Guide)

As the year unfolds, many people like you will be making resolutions they want to achieve over the next 12 months or for the coming years. Most may never succeed without the right techniques. Let this book cut down your learning time by teaching you a few principles that will ensure your New Year's Resolutions succeed!

Book Title: How To Raise Money For Your Business: The Ultimate Guide For Start Up Businesses; Book

If you want to know the truth about raising money for your business this book is for you.

If you are having a tough time raising the money you want for your business this book is for you too.

If you are not sure where to go to get the kind of funding you need for your business this book is just what you need.

After many years of helping businesses of various kinds raise the money they want, I have laid out in print all that you need to know about raising money for your start-up business! .

Made in United States
North Haven, CT
14 August 2025

71701707R00036